LONELY LINES

A COLLECTION OF PROSE AND POETRY

By

FREYA O'BRIEN

First Printing, 2022

ISBN-13: 978-1-73933-9-5 (sc)
ISBN-13: 978-1-73933-7-1 (eb)

Hello,

My name is Freya and welcome to my first book of poetry.

I am sharing personal experiences through my poems, to help those going through similar things feel less alone. The poems cover heavy topics, and therefore I recommend dipping in and out of my book when you feel like you have the mental and emotional space to do so.

You may relate to a few poems; you may relate to all of them. Either way, I hope you enjoy reading my poems and find the experience validating.

I was lost in a sea

Of overwhelming pain,

Fighting being consumed by misery,

Whilst my heart was being slain.

And yet, in the darkness,

I find accidental muses.

My pen glides across the page,

Filled with grief and my bruises.

To my amazing partner
James – for being my
light in the darkest
of times. *I love you*.

TABLE OF CONTENTS

9   FAMILY

45   RELATIONSHIPS

TABLE OF CONTENTS

81   MENTAL HEALTH & LIFE

117   ABOUT FREYA

FAMILY

Flour covers the counters,
Our faces and hair.
Laughter fills the house,
We make quite the pair!

We mix the ingredients
And bake the cake.
Licking the bowl and spoons
Whilst we wait.

We prepare the icing
And decorations.
Enjoying a family activity
Passed down for generations.

My mum rolls the icing
And creates the shapes.
I am in awe
Of what she creates.

I don't actually mind
What we are baking,
All that matters are the memories
We are creating.

Her embrace was home,
Her laughter contagious,
She was my role model,
Her strength was endless.

She wiped away tears,
And made every day special
Just by being here.
Her presence was essential.

When she passed away,
I was so young.
It felt like someone had ripped out
My heart and my tongue.

I couldn't speak
Or feel anymore.
It took many years
For my heart to restore.

Mum, I miss you dearly.

I walk down memory lane
Because I love running into you.
You smile, laugh and hug me.
We talk for ages too.

If only I could see you
One last time,
Instead of replaying old memories
In this head of mine.

13

I sat by my bedroom window, looking out at the tree in the front garden, watching it move gracefully in the wind. My hair cascades down my face, my eyes glistening and tears sticking to my cheeks. I don't make a single sound as tears fall around me. I hug my knees to my chest like they are a friend. My only comfort. I continue to admire how free the tree is and alas continue to be reminded how much I crave my own freedom.

My stepmothers voice beckons me from downstairs, ripping me away from the tree. I wipe my tears, put my glasses on and rush downstairs. She doesn't look at me or acknowledge my presence, but her hand waves in the direction of the kitchen. I follow the direction; she doesn't even have to say what she wants out loud anymore. The direction and expectation I have every day and have had for years - to cook dinner for everyone, a household of five.

I open the fridge and my eyes glide over the ingredients. I take out what I need and head over to the counter. I prepare the ingredients, careful not to make too much noise to avoid confrontation as my stepmother looks on. I prepare the meal and clean the kitchen as its cooking. Another expectation and rule they have set for me, to keep the house spotless.

I hear the key turn in the front door. My father is home. His footsteps echo across the hall, his "Hello" loud and authoritative. My heart races as I set the dinner out. He doesn't say thank you, in fact he doesn't say anything to me. He talks to my stepmother like I am invisible. Oh, how I wish that to be the case.

My stepmother calls my sister and stepsister down from their bedrooms. I hear their laughter and joy spread through the house as they open their doors and end their phone calls with their friends. They come down the stairs and sit down.

Again, I'm not invited or welcome to sit with them. I walk out of the kitchen and go back to my bedroom. My stepmother or father will call me when they are done.

I plop back onto my bed in a room that's so small it holds just a bed and a wardrobe, and the door opens into the only floor space left. I open my school bag and lift out my homework. I find solace in my essays, my pen gliding over the paper with my words, rapidly filling the pages.

Alas, the sounds of plates and cutlery being set down at the table ring throughout the house and pierce through me. Even though no one says anything, I know it's my cue to come downstairs to clear them. I sigh and wonder how this has happened, how have I been lumbered with all these chores and expectations whilst the rest of my family relax in the lounge - their laughter echoing across the house.

A PARENT

A parent is meant to be a safe space,
Not someone I'm scared to look in the face.

A parent is meant to show affection,
Not act cold and bark orders with conviction.

A parent is meant to meet my basic needs,
Not with mouldy food and a house full of weeds.

A parent is meant to prepare me for adult life,
But not through neglect, hardship and strife.

A parent is meant to love and care for their child,
And I can't understand why you don't.
It drives me wild.

WHY

Why doesn't my dad love me?
Why doesn't he at least speak to me?
Why does he no longer see me?
I'm starting to think the problem lies with me.

As these thoughts take over my head,
I feel the pain of rejection start
to spread.

18

VILE REALITY

My dreams scream,
My heart aches,
My soul burns
From what reality takes.

This vile reality
Of endless loss and pain,
Changes me forever.
I will never be the same.

I was struggling at school,
I was struggling at home,
Everything felt too much
And I felt so alone.

I tried to handle the grief
And the overwhelming pain,
But anything I did had no impact,
Those feelings stayed the same.

I asked my dad for counselling
And he got right up in my face,
Saying I didn't need to go
Because that would be a disgrace.

It was the first thing I had asked of him
In a very long time,
I realised I'd never get what I needed
From that dad of mine.

So, I bottled everything up,
And kept it all inside,
Learning to smile through the pain
I gradually learned to hide.

Until I no longer felt anything,
But incredibly numb.
Over time, I no longer noticed
How detached I had become.

From a young age
You taught me love had to be earned.
That I wasn't wanted unless I was useful.
Oh, how your distance burned.

Your lack of empathy and emotion,
Your cold, calculated moves,
All felt like we were playing a game
Designed for me to lose.

I left home at eighteen,
Without a penny to my name.
I couldn't stay at home much longer,
It was driving me insane.

I felt like I couldn't make a move
Or even speak,
Because they changed their expectations
And rules every week.

They made their rules up
On the spot,
To always catch me in the "wrong".
It was a lot.

I faced constant criticism
For minor things,
And they were enraged
If I ever shared my feelings.

So, I learned to bottle everything up inside.
And when I finally felt safe, I realised how much of me
had died.

You broke my spirit, shattered my heart and cursed my very soul.

Waves of overwhelming pain course their way through my body.

I am drowning, floundering, gasping, thrashing around
Trying to desperately stay afloat.

Until I get tired,

I no longer want to swim and fight through this immense current,

I just want it to end.

And with that I am swept under,

Deep within the dark abyss of the sea.

Grief, rejection and pain swirling around me in strong currents.

My lungs are burning from the saltwater rising up inside,

I am gasping for breath, for peace in all this pain.

I thrash around desperately looking for the surface, for a miracle to come and save me.

For the ocean to suddenly spit me out.

But nothing happens.

I continue to sink further and further into the darkest of waters.

Until I realise that I am dying.

My very soul wants to live but sees no other way out.

But I am dying.

My very being is dying.

I cannot give up so easily.

I need to fight through this.

I am a fighter.

I can get through this.

I stop thrashing around.

I stop breathing in the burning water.

I

just

Stop.

The water calms around me just enough to see what appears to be the surface.

I'll take that chance.

But how do I swim whilst my very limbs are tired, whilst my lungs are oozing with salt water and my brain is exploding with a lack of air.

How do I get there?

I am ashamed of how deep the water has pushed me down.

I am embarrassed and hate myself for allowing myself to sink so far.

I do not want to admit to myself that I need help

That I need to tell someone.

The words are fighting to stay within me.

Swirling around my heart and mind.

I do not trust my judgements.

I do not trust myself.

I hate how I have gotten myself here.

I fight the urge to breathe in the burning salt water one last time,

And scream with all my might.
I scream with everything I have.
Trying to push the words out,
Trying to get someone to notice,
Trying to apologise,
Trying to get help,
All at once,
In this enduring scream.
And with that,
This beacon suddenly turns on.
This light radiates down to the very depth of my heart and mind.
My limbs start to move.
One in front of the other.
Slowly,
Hesitantly at first.
Until I realise the beacon is from those who care,
Those who I have hurt but still want to help.
My strokes get bigger and more powerful.
I fight the oxygen-less cells wanting to give up.
I power through to meet them halfway,
And I am engulfed in a warm hug.
The warmth seeps into my cold skin,
Giving me some relief from the cold waters that float within me.
A hand is extended to me and pulls me up to the surface so I can breathe.
I cough up the wretched salt water.
I warm up my body with hugs from the ones I love.

I look around.

I apologise to those who were trying to reach out whilst I was in the deepest of waters.

Those I simply couldn't see through the swirling water of pain inside.

I try to make amends.

I look further.

Trying to see where I am.

Trying to work out how to get back to shore.

Trying to piece together my sense of self.

Trying to work out how I got here.

Simple.

The pain of immense grief of losing something so fundamental as a father's and sister's love, pushed me deep under water, engulfing me in pain and emotion. In unbearable grief and rejection.

I will need to take each day as it comes.

One day at a time.

Until I feel like there is enough space from the ocean of pain and me.

Until I can say "it is sad that things are the way they are, that I lost my father and sister so young and felt so much pain that I was swept away by it. But I fought through it, and it made me stronger".

I can do this.

I will do this.

I can get there.

After I left home,
And left the toxicity behind,
They would still try to reach out
Just to be unkind.

My step-mum sent texts to say
How much better they were without me.
Maybe this was her plan all along,
And my absence filled her with glee.

My dad however
Doesn't talk to me anymore.
He sent a Christmas card years ago,
But I just wondered what for.

They know I'm getting married next year,
And that I've been in hospital recently.
But surprise, surprise,
They have not messaged me.

Will they ever reach out again?
I do not know.
But if I had to place my bets,
I would say no.

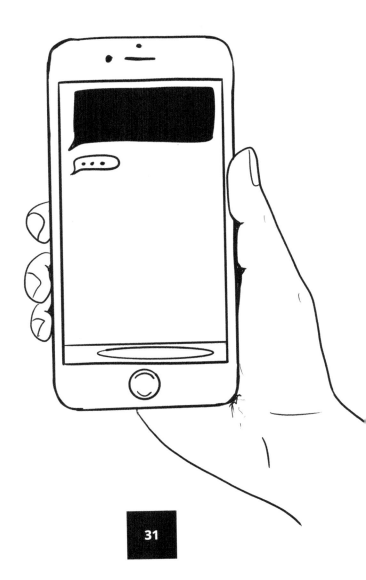

Growing up, they used to say
"Blood is thicker than water",
But you were never there
For your own daughter.

Your absence and distance
Weighed on me heavily,
Because you did not show
Any care or love for me.

You don't deserve
To be called "Dad".
You never fulfilled that role,
And that makes me mad.

Family to me is more than
Blood and DNA.
It's truly being there,
Not this foul play.

It's the friends and family
Who have been there through it all,
Even when I thought
My pain was too tall.

They've helped me to bandage
And repair emotional scars.
They have helped me so much,
And to me, they are the true stars.

After all these years,
Do you think of me dad?
Does not being in my life
At least make you feel sad?

Or am I nothing to you?
You don't care at all.
I'm just a distant memory,
You no longer recall.

Growing up, I always wanted the perfect family
And a loving house with a white picket fence.
It was the dream sold in movies,
And coming from a broken home, it made sense.

However, now that I'm actually considering
Starting a family of my own.
I'm learning that my biggest fear
Is repeating the behaviours I was shown.

I don't want to recreate a house
Made of eggshells and glass,
Scared of making a move or speaking,
Whilst maintaining a happy home farce.

I want them to feel safe, happy
And loved at their core.
Instead of getting scared of the footsteps
At their door.

What if I can't have kids.
What if my womb
Is never more than
An empty room.

What if I can't
carry a child,
And the idea of surrogacy
Drives me wild.

What if I can't
Stomach the cost of IVF,
What other options
Would we have left.

What if I am open
To look at adoption,
But my partner isn't open
To considering that option.

What if I can't have kids, and we veto all our options.
Would my partner have doubts, and reconsiderations?

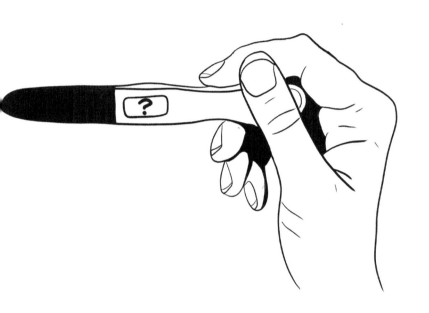

When that positive sign
Appeared on the test,
I was elated and happy,
And surprised I rightly guessed.

It felt like all my dreams had finally come true,
And yet it hit me, maybe all my fears would too.

I didn't want to repeat my experiences,
And have my child feel neglected.
I wanted them to always feel loved,
Cared for and protected.

As I cradled my stomach,
And thought of my growing child,
I couldn't ever imagine treating them
Like you treated me,
And that makes me so riled.

I tried to shake your shadow
And memories out of my brain,
So, I could enjoy my pregnancy
Despite my emotional pain.

I promised to be the parent I needed as a child,
And to heal my old scars.
So, my child can be happy, healthy
And reach for the stars.

Midwives and doctors, do not rush me.
I want to give birth with dignity.
I am not a burden or a vessel!
I am a birthing mother, do not make me wrestle
Just to feel safe, settled and heard.
Be my safe place, this is absurd!

Guide me through this labour,
Do not act like this is a favour.
I am vulnerable and scared, please this is too much to bear.
Stop being so scary and pushy, I think I'm only being fair
To ask you to stop acting like I'm a child
This is making me feel so riled!

Give me the autonomy and authority over my body.
Your lack of care is really shoddy.
Stop and think about what you are doing.
I am more than just a body you are viewing.

Do better.

You may be my parent,
But I am theirs.
Stop with the ifs, buts,
Complaining and stares.

You need to respect
My parental decisions.
Instead of bombarding me
With suggested revisions.

I appreciate your support
And everything you've done for me.
But please, unless I ask for advice,
Let my decisions be.

Her eyes held such innocence
When she looked at me.
I wanted to shield her
From how cruel the world can be.

When I was a child,
I was forced to grow up fast.
I will do everything I can
To keep that cycle in the past.

She deserves a happy
Childhood and life,
Instead of facing such
Hardship and strife.

She reached out,
Her fingers curling around mine.
I knew from that moment,
I'd protect her for all of time.

RELATIONSHIPS

When I became interested in dating,
Your actions were all I knew of love.
My first relationships were toxic,
And absent of the care I felt unworthy of.

I craved love and attention,
From anyone and any source.
Putting myself in toxic situations,
With those who have no remorse.

I convinced myself I liked anyone
Who gave me the smallest time of day,
Because I hadn't felt wanted in so long.
But they didn't ever stay.

They preyed on my need for love,
Like predators and their prey.
They could sense I was an easy target
From a mile away.

After a while, I realised
I had broken my heart time and time again,
Trying to mend old scars and wounds
With loveless relationships with men.

Finally, I decided to stop.
Stop this endless, toxic cycle.
Stop looking for love in all the wrong places.
It really was quite the debacle.

I had to learn what was toxic,
And what was okay.
To take the time to heal old wounds,
So, I could be happy someday.

A FAIRY-TALE

Today was a fairy-tale,
Or so I once thought.
Now I see your hidden games,
And the feelings you never caught.

"You looked better with your t-shirt on"
Is what he said to me
After I had slept with him for the first time,
And lost my virginity.

He then got up and left me alone
Allowing his words to fester inside.
My first serious relationship down the drain,
As I realised a part of me had died.

A partner is meant to lift you up,
Support you and add to your life,
Not make you feel awful about yourself
And create inner strife.

His cold, heartless words
Taught me a lesson that night.
I will not tolerate this behaviour,
I deserve a partner that treats me right.

I used to believe in fairy tales,
And Prince Charming.
That's why meeting you,
Was very disarming.

I thought you were my prince,
My happy ever after.
But we didn't even get past,
The very first chapter.

You managed to break my heart
And create emotional scars,
Whilst I still had my head in the clouds,
High enough to see stars.

However, I won't let your chapter end my love story
Before it's even begun,
Because whilst you were good for the plot line,
You are not the one.

Do I taste the deceit on your lips,
The trace of her on your fingertips?

Do I see it in your eyes,
When you tell me all these lies?

You say I'm crazy, and that nothing is going on.
But I know it has, I just don't know for how long.

He doesn't hit me,
He punches walls instead.
But how long will it be
Until his fist meets my head.

He doesn't hit me,
But I always step back,
Waiting and preparing
For his next attack.

He doesn't hit me,
But I can't have a say.
Anytime I try to,
He shouts at me all day.

I need to stop excusing his behaviour,
When violence is how he will return the favour.

I'm not seeing red flags,
But am I seeing pink?
It's so hard to know
What to really think.

You shower me with flowers,
Words of love and romance,
Isn't it a bit too much, too fast
To do this love-bomb dance.

You don't take photos of us,
And we haven't got a label,
Are you still keeping other options
On the table?

I haven't met your friends and family,
And yet you've met mine.
Are we just in different places,
And this will be fine?

CONSENT

A yes out of fear or to shut you up is NOT consent.
Just because you brought me a drink or dinner,
Does not mean I owe you anything.
You are acting like you've paid my body's rent,
But there is no such thing.
Stop pestering!

Your blood burns inside
And stains a crimson red.
Everything was robbed from you
In this empty bed.

You lie there feeling broken,
Used and disheartened,
Whilst you know he has left
To live his life unburdened.

You never tell anyone
Or report this awful crime,
Because who would believe
You didn't consent at the time.

If you walk alone at night, you wanted it.
If you drink, you wanted it.
If you go to his house, you wanted it.
If you even look at him once, you wanted it.

"You wanted it" is what they all say
To women simply going about their day.
We get taught not to be a target,
Instead of teaching men not to do it.

If this was any other crime, we would not blame the victim,
And yet here they all are siding with him.

Quick movements,
Men running towards or past me,
Raised voices,
And being touched anywhere on my body.

A hug from a family member
Was no longer safe or calming.
I felt like I couldn't breathe.
It was all so alarming.

I saw you in men's faces everywhere,
And I no longer felt safe anywhere.

I see you in strangers faces,
And in recurring dreams,
But only when my stress and pain
Are bursting at the seams.

Like a sickening alarm bell
Ringing from my brain,
You are now an unsettling warning
That I'm feeling too much pain.

You burn in my mind
And own my breath.
My lungs gasp and burn,
As my mind asks for death.

But, there has to be more,
More than this endless pain.
More than this experience.
All men just can't be the same.

LOVING YOU WAS RED

My heart sang when we were together,
But my blood boiled when we ended.
Loving you was red, raw and angry
As your actions were defended.

You were like a raging,
All-consuming fire.
A mysterious soul
That awakened my desire.

However, you wanted to run free,
And not be contained.
The tighter I held on,
The more we became strained.

I realised the longer
I tried to stop you,
The more I hurt
And burned both of us too.

We didn't work out,
And that's okay.
I deserve someone
Who wants to stay.

ASHES

We fight, we burn
Like a bonfire of chaos.
Each trying to love
Whilst trying to be the boss.

We burn each other to ashes.

Collecting hearts is your favourite past time,
Promising the world but not giving a dime.

Showing off your conquests to your mates over beer,
Comparing recent exploits with a wink and sneer.

Do you really feel so empty and needy for attention,
That you'd rather use your body to get people to listen.

Why don't you start valuing yourself more?
You can start by showing these sordid behaviours the door.

I'm like a tiger watching their prey,
Every time I catch you in your lie of the day.

Your lies fill the air like a swarm of flies.
Every time you speak, a part of me dies.

I wait until you feel like I believe you,
Until I pounce and let your backtracking ensue.

Your words mean nothing to me anymore.
I say we are through and settle the score.

You're out late with the guys,
And I'm home alone.
For some reason,
You're not picking up your phone.

My mind automatically races
And assumes the worst;
That you're cheating on me
And my relationships are cursed.

I know this is my previous relationships talking,
But that doesn't stop the fear of you walking.

The warmth of your embrace is craved,
As winters chill cuts deep into my skin.
You're an absence that aches
And rots my heart from within.

The price of love is worth it,
Or so they all said.
But I'm not so sure,
Now that I'm exploding with heartbreak instead.

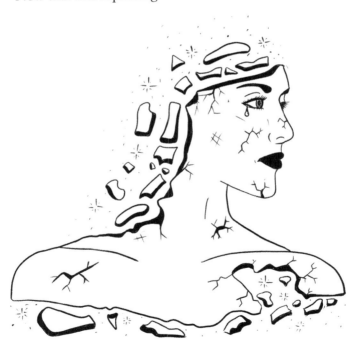

DESIRE

Our desire for each other
Burns strong and fast,
But does this mean
We will not last?

You were like the coldest winter,
Stubborn, ferociously bitter,
Distant and heartless.
I had to reconsider.

Your behaviour and lack of warmth
Was slowly killing my soul.
I didn't want to be like you,
I wanted my heart to be whole.

I want to love, laugh and be happy
Instead of cold, haggard and snappy.

As soon as we ended,
My heart danced and bloomed.
I could finally grow
Beyond where you loomed.
My heart and soul finally healed,
And I changed the cards you had dealt.

My heart feels exhausted and burned from betrayal.
It feels like just one more heartbreak could be fatal.

I'll build up strong walls and defences around my heart.
So, it won't be so easy for anyone else to tear me apart.

Those who deserve my heart, love and time
Will be willing to scale the walls and make the climb.

I will call the walls "standards" from now on,
I think I've just been settling for far too long.

You shut yourself away
In your office or our bedroom,
Always choosing to withdraw
And spend time alone.

Do you think you don't need to invest
In our relationship?
Or do you not care about me at all,
Am I just a passing ship?

You used to be my lover,
In a very distant spring.
Now, you are just a memory
Of a past summer fling.

If I saw you on the street,
Would we even say hi,
Or would we be forgotten lovers
Simply passing each other by.

I used to look for love
In all the wrong places,
Thinking I wanted any guy
Who gave me glances.

I was so used to being ignored
And love deprived,
I craved it from everyone
And anyone who tried.

I got lost for a while
In toxic relationships,
Trying to make them work
But they were just blips.

You see I didn't really want
Those I was with.
I just wanted a relationship
To give me enough "love" to live.

But I don't regret my past,
It was survival.
I realise now my way of coping
Slowly became my rival.

Now, I value myself
A hell of a lot more,
And I'm with someone
I love and adore.

My darkest of days
Are always brighter
When you hold me close
And hug me tighter

Your presence soothes
The raging storm inside
And I feel at home
With you by my side

Thank you for being there for me
I love you to infinity

Butterflies fluttered in my stomach
Electricity danced through me
The world seemed so much brighter
I had never felt so free

Your calming eyes and kind smile
Decorated your handsome face
And made me feel instantly at home
I never wanted to leave our embrace

I knew from the moment we met
You were the one for me
You are my soulmate, best friend, partner
And now husband to be

I love you

MINE

Your lips tasted of red wine
Our limbs passionately intertwine
Today was a fairy-tale or storyline
As we lovingly called each other "mine"

MENTAL HEALTH & LIFE

THE FLY

Poor mental health
Is like a fly
You can't swat away.
No matter how hard you try.

Just this constant
Buzzing in your brain
And after a while
You feel your energy wane.

You just want a break
From this incessant noise,
But you're expected to handle it
With grace and poise.

Sometimes the fly goes for some time,
But never for long enough to actually feel fine.

Sometimes, your only friends
Are the tears on your cheeks,
And the bed you haven't
Managed to leave in weeks.

You are too numb
And tired from the pain,
That trying to feel anything else
Is in vain.

And you don't have the energy
To reach out.
All you do is question
And fill your thoughts with doubt.

Living feels like too much energy,
But you don't want to die.
You just want to lie here
And watch the days go by.

The familiar burning sensation
Glides down my throat.
This liquor stops my troubles
Like a magical cloak.

I no longer feel burdened
By the woes of the day.
I feel like I always want
Things to be this way.

However, as soon as I'm sober
My world comes crashing down.
I feel so dark and empty inside,
My smile turns into a frown.

And so back to drinking I go,
To combat feeling so low.

One glass, two glasses, three glasses, four.
I don't feel my troubles anymore.

Five glasses, six glasses, seven glasses, eight.
I'm starting to get myself into a state.

Nine glasses, ten glasses. I'm on the floor!
I promise myself I won't drink anymore.

The next day rolls around and I do it again.
I realise I'm drinking all the time, instead of now and then.

ALCOHOL DEPENDENCY SELF HELP

(This is what worked for me, not medical advice.

Set a limit. This can be a couple of drinks or zero (T-Total)

Remove all alcohol from the house

Tell trusted friends and family for support

When out, have soda or mocktails if you want a drink

Seek counselling for the deeper issues

Alcohol dependency was hard to shake,
I felt like I couldn't get through the days without a drink.
It took me getting into accidents and breaking bones,
To realise my mental health was at the brink.

I had to stop drinking, but how I wondered.
I barely got through the day with the energy I mustered.

Until one day, I said enough was enough.
I couldn't keep drinking like I was an endless pit,
I had to stop this now
Before the drinking destroys me where I sit.

I promised myself I wouldn't do this anymore.
It was hard and such a struggle to stay on track.
But I did it. I kept my promise.
And now I feel like I have my life back.

You know that feeling
When the world weighs on you.
When you feel crushed,
And struggle to think too.

When the world seems so dark,
And you can't feel happy.
When all you want to do is cry
And you feel so crappy.

When everything is too much
And you can't see your future,
And you don't feel like you can
Drag yourself any further.

Please know that you are not alone,
People do care about you.
They can help you through this
And carry the weight too.

I promise you
It will get better.
Even if it doesn't feel like it,
We can get through this together.

All is not lost,
It will be okay.
You will see,
When you look back on this someday.

I hid my pain and grief in many bottles
I've kept squirreled away.
Never opening them up or acknowledging them,
Always keeping the pain at bay.

I was never shown how to feel
Or process my emotions in a healthy way.
I was taught my feelings were invalid
And so, I've kept them buried to this day.

But the feelings started oozing out of their bottles,
And exploding out of me.
I had no choice but to feel the pain,
I could no longer leave it be.

I never allowed myself to feel or grieve,
Because I thought it would destroy me.
But I've realised the opposite it true
And allowing myself to feel the pain
Is finally setting me free.

I can see it on your face
That it is tough,
And no amount of reassurance
Will ever be enough.

You feel lost, anxious
And overwhelmed
By all the thoughts and feeling
You have withheld.

You are trying to process
Too much at once,
From all the pain and emotions
You've kept bottled for months.

But it will be okay.
You will get through this, my dear.
Your thoughts and feelings are valid,
And not something to fear.

I struggle with balance,
It's all or nothing with me.
I can't do middle ground,
I find it impossible to see.

I either restrict my eating,
Or eat the entire house.
I either feel confident
Or as quiet as a mouse.

I either have an exercise regime,
Or I'm a couch potato.
I either shop until I drop,
Or have a budget of zero.

I'm like a two-sided coin,
Being flipped over and over again.
But I can't control it,
I just switch modes every now and then.

THE MOUSE

Where has my confidence gone?
I feel like a mouse,
Struggling to speak
When I'm not in my house.

I struggle in meetings
And in groups too.
Oh confidence, where have you gone?
I really need you!

I feel so upset.
I don't want to be here.
I want to be home,
Away from this fear.

Oh gosh, why can't I say a word.
It's almost like I don't want to be heard.

I felt like I couldn't breathe,
Like the world was closing in,
Like I was going to vomit,
From the anxiety rising within.

ANXIETY GROUNDING TECHNIQUE

Focus on your breathing, then identify

5 things you can see

3 things you can hear

4 things you can touch

2 things you can smell

1 thing you can taste

Do you know what's disgraceful?
I have been convinced that I am unworthy,
Unworthy of merely existing,
By strangers, lovers and some family.

How can something so fundamental as living
Be put into question.
It's shocking and heart-breaking
That I've felt so invalid, because of them.

Because of them, I've said sorry a thousand times
For simply being.
Because of them, I've never truly cared for myself
Or my wellbeing.

And now I'm at breaking point,
Not knowing how to fix what's broken,
Because how do you find the "you" you once knew,
The "you" they have taken?

I am lost, I feel empty.
I just want to re-find "me".

I've kept my head down
For the entire year.
Not allowing myself to grieve
Or shed a single tear.

I've tried to keep going
And appear like my normal self.
But all I've done is harm,
By putting my feelings on a shelf.

I'm now at the end of the year,
Looking up for the first time
And all I can see is the damage I've done
By ignoring these feelings of mine.

Grief is pouring out of me.
My heart and soul feel broken.
But I've got to feel in order to heal,
My heart and body have spoken.

So here I am at breaking point,
Finally advocating for myself.
Taking the time I need to process everything,
I once put on a shelf.

You feel like you're messed up from trauma
And years of abuse.
But that does not mean you can hurt others,
There is no excuse.

Take responsibility for healing
Your emotional wounds that bleed.
It's not right to cover others in your blood,
Are we agreed?

People think self-care is candles,
Shopping, face masks,
Bubble baths and spas.
Simply a collection of beauty tasks.

But self-care is so much more.
It's saying "no", taking breaks,
Going to therapy,
And healing from life's mistakes.

Self-care isn't always comfortable,
It's valuing and healing yourself when you are able.

I lost my way
For many years.
I felt so numb,
I had no more tears.

I just felt empty
And like I no longer cared.
No longer valuing my life,
Or so I declared.

I drank a lot
To ease the pain,
But no matter what
I felt the same.

It wasn't until
I saw a therapist,
That I started seeing the me
I really missed.

Whilst the journey wasn't comfortable,
Or easy.
In the end, healing the wounds
Set me free.

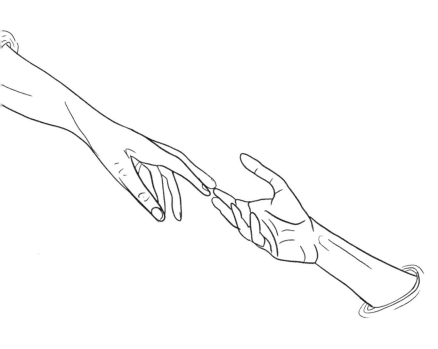

Hearts break,
Tears stream and fall.
The agonising pain of healing,
And mending it all.

Worth it.

VALID FEELINGS

Everything you feel is valid,
You are allowed to have feelings.
At the end of the day,
We are all human beings.

Anyone who says that you are overreacting,
Doesn't deserve a moment of your time, my darling.

Commenting on someone's weight
Thinking its constructive or complimentary,
Is not okay or your right.
It's really rudimentary.

These comments perpetuate
A weight stigma culture,
Unhealthy relationships with our bodies
And us feeling vulgar.

It's not your place,
Or okay to say
"You've gained weight"
Or "you look okay"

No one has the right to comment on size.
Our bodies do not exist solely for your eyes.

I truly looked at myself
For the first time.
I studied my body,
Every shape and every line.

I appreciated my body
In its current state,
Trying to stop being cruel
And become my own mate.

I stood in front of the mirror
Trying to be grateful
For my wonderful body,
To which I've been spiteful.

I now list the things I love
About this body of mine
And this continues to grow,
More and more with time.

I want to throw my hands up in the air
And jump for joy.
I want to celebrate my successes
Without the pressure to be coy.

We are taught to be modest
And refuse compliments.
To stand there and accept others' words
As they leave their dents.

But I will not downplay my value anymore
To appease small-minded businessmen.
Those who are threatened by my existence,
Should just jog on then.

My hands are up in the air,
I'm unapologetically here,
And anyone who disagrees with that
Should simply disappear.

I've finally realised
I won't get what I need from others.
I need to provide it myself,
And that's why my heart suffers.

I've been looking for love,
Validation and purpose externally.
Instead of in self-love,
Acceptance and wants internally.

I've been craving others approval
For so long.
I've forgotten myself
And my heart's song.

I don't know how to love myself
Or where to start.
I guess I'll stop listening to others
And stop tearing myself apart.

I'll also try new things
Like self-compassion and forgiveness,
And let go of the pain of the past
And all that makes me grimace.

Here's to me, finally trying to be me.

You are valued and enough,
Just as you are.
You don't need a fancy house,
Or a posh car.

You don't need a degree
From a top university,
Or a high-flying job
In the middle of the city.

You don't need to be skinny,
Or a certain size.
Or be awarded a certificate,
Or a grand prize.

You are valued and enough, just as you are.
You are worthy of your dreams, and you can go far.

Don't let me be misunderstood.
Let my voice ring across the mountains,
Let my heart dance and bloom,
Let my mind flow like fountains,
Let my uniqueness be free,
For there is only one me.

**THANK YOU
FOR READING**

ABOUT FREYA

Freya O'Brien is an English poet and illustrator who channels her heart through her pen. She creates poems and illustrations based on her personal life, thoughts and emotions.

Freya uses a pen and paper as an outlet on the darkest of days, to celebrate life, and connect with those who may be able to relate.

Find Freya on Instagram

@lonelylines.poetry

www.lonelylinespoetry.co.uk

Printed in Great Britain
by Amazon

81430269R00072